*70*
# COMMON CACTI
# OF THE SOUTHWEST

# 70 COMMON CACTI

## OF THE SOUTHWEST

Pierre C. Fischer

SOUTHWEST PARKS AND MONUMENTS ASSOCIATION
TUCSON, ARIZONA

© Copyright 1989 by Southwest Parks and Monuments Association
ISBN 0-911408-82-7
Library of Congress Number 89-061677

Editorial: T.J. Priehs, Carolyn Dodson
Design: Christina Watkins
Production: Nancy Curtis, Christina Watkins
Lithography: Lorraine Press, Inc., Salt Lake City, Utah

All photographs by Pierre C. Fischer except as credited.

Cover photograph: *Opuntia basilaris* (John Cacheris)

1st printing, 12/89 20,000
2nd printing 5/91 20,000

# INTRODUCTION

Members of the cactus family have been of considerable interest to plant lovers as well as botanists because of their strange shapes, spines, and showy flowers. Although they are now distributed around the world, all except four tropical species are native only to the Americas. Most have fleshy or succulent stems; certainly all those occurring naturally in the United States are stem succulents with very little woody tissues except for tall species and chollas.

Some of the tropical cacti have large leaves which in most cases are fleshy. Those native to this country never have leaves on mature growth, although tiny leaves that soon dry up develop on the newly formed stems of *Opuntia*.

Spines, which are believed to have evolved from leaves, grow in clusters (figure 2) within specialized areas called areoles (figure 1). Spines are frequently of two kinds: centrals which are heavier, more deeply pigmented and often hooked; and radials, almost always straight, that are disposed around the centrals.

Areoles, from which branches and flowers usually originate, are distributed in a regular manner along the stems and many have felt and long hairs in addition to spines.

While the stems of some cacti are ribbed (fluted), others have protuberances called tubercles. In those cacti with tubercles, the spine bearing areoles are located at their tips. The tubercles of some species are grooved on their upper surfaces, the grooves being an extension of the areole (figure 3).

It is scarcely possible to distinguish between sepals and petals of the flowers in this family as these gradually change from one to the other, green to brightly colored. These perianth parts and the numerous stamens are united at their bases into a floral tube which varies in length from one species to another. The tube in turn arises from the ovary which forms the lowest part of the flower (figure 4). The ovary, where the seeds develop and which becomes the fruit, may be spiny, hairy, scaly or smooth.

Cacti, as every group of living organisms, show a certain amount of variation from individual to individual. For that reason you should not expect every plant of a given species to look exactly alike, e.g. spines may vary somewhat in length or color.

Only commonly occurring cacti have been described in this book. For those readers who desire a complete treatment of the cacti of the Southwest, I recommend one of the books mentioned in the reading list.

Newcomers to the Southwest will want to know which plants may be confused with cacti:

Century plants (*Agave*) and hen-and-chicks (*Dudleya, Echeveria, Graptopetalum*) whose succulent leaves are in the form of a rosette are not cacti. Nor are *Yuccas*, sotol (*Dasylirion*), bear-grass (*Nolina*), and the desert pineapple (*Hechtia*) that have long leathery leaves. The ocotillo (*Fouquieria splendens*) has long wand-like spiny branches, is woody and has normal looking leaves that appear only after a rain. The only stem succulent which is not a cactus is the candelilla (*Euphorbia antisyphilitica*). It is a low plant of many, slender, crowded, gray-green branches which bear no spines nor areoles; its flowers are minute. It is found almost exclusively in the Big Bend region of Texas, and in Mexico.

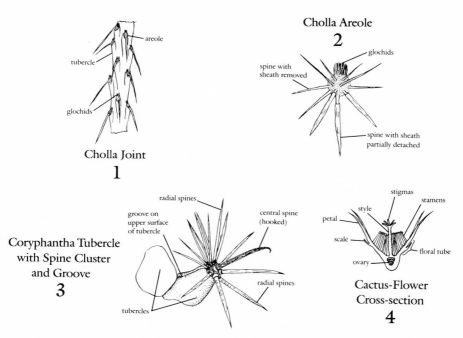

Cholla Areole
2

Cholla Joint
1

Coryphantha Tubercle
with Spine Cluster
and Groove
3

Cactus-Flower
Cross-section
4

---

# DESERTS

A biologist defines a desert as a region where annual precipitation is low and irregular in its occurrence. Often this aridity is accompanied by high summer temperatures. In a desert, plants grow distant from one another due to root competition for scarce water and frequently the vegetation is of low stature.

The type of vegetation of a given desert depends not only on the amount of precipitation but also in what season of the year it comes. A given amount of rain during cool weather will be more effective than during hot weather. Low winter temperatures occurring in some deserts will also influence what plants will live there.

Deserts may exist at low or high elevations depending on the local topography and climatic conditions of the region. As you travel from the desert to higher elevations precipitation increases and temperature drops, so that gradually the vegetation changes and the desert gives way to some other plant community such as grassland or chaparral (closely spaced, low shrubs mostly with evergreen leaves).

North of Palm Springs and Joshua Tree National Monument is the Mojave Desert. On its western edge it receives only winter rains but towards its eastern boundary, in Arizona, it may get some summer precipitation. Most of the Mojave Desert lies at high elevation and is cold in winter. Much of this desert is dry and barren, and it is only in its less arid parts that one finds the Joshua Tree which is a species of yucca, found nowhere else. Cacti are few here.

Along the Mexican border in California and western Arizona, is the Colorado Desert (a subdivision of the Sonoran Desert), where rainfall is restricted to the winter months. Because of its low elevation, temperatures are high and rainfall very low. As a consequence of these climatic extremes, vegetation is sparse and there are few cacti.

Farther east, in the Arizona Desert (another subdivision of the Sonoran Desert) summer precipitation increases, and in Sonora, Mexico, summer rains are most important. This is probably the most spectacular desert in this country, and is often called an arborescent desert because it contains a high proportion of tall plants (small trees, yuccas and giant cacti such as the saguaro). This large number of arborescent species is made possible by the bimodal rainfall and relatively high temperatures both in summer and winter. Cacti, large and small, are plentiful in this desert.

Rain in the form of summer thunderstorms is the principal source of precipitation in the Chihuahuan Desert. Although this comparatively high desert is most extensive in Mexico, it reaches into west Texas, southern New Mexico, and a small region of southeastern Arizona. Its vegetation consists of shrubs, yuccas, agaves, and a great many small cacti.

Since some of the deserts described here extend into Mexico, many of the cacti mentioned in this book also grow south of the border.

The geographical area covered in this book corresponds roughly to the Mojave, Colorado, Arizona, and Chihuahuan Deserts as shown on the map, as well as that part of southeastern Arizona that lies between the Arizona and Chihuahuan Deserts.

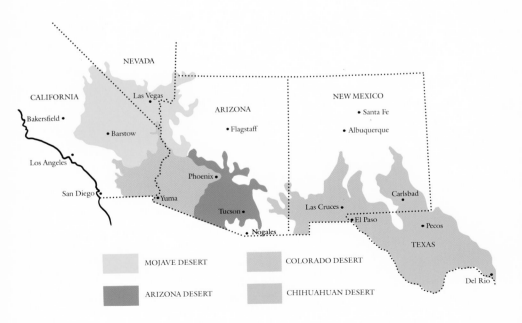

# OPUNTIA
## *(Prickly Pears and Chollas)*

Unlike most other cacti, chollas and prickly pears are many-branched, each branch arising from another as in a tree. The branches or "joints" of chollas are more or less cylindrical, and in most species covered with elongated protuberances called tubercles. Prickly pear branches, often called pads, are flattened and look like overgrown, fleshy leaves. Only chollas have papery sheaths covering their spines; these are often showy and bright, thus giving the plant its overall coloration.

In addition to the regular large spines found on most cacti, chollas and prickly pears bear clusters of easily detached tiny, yellow to red spines called glochids, that are found just above the ordinary spine cluster (figure 3). Since these glochids are barbed and almost too small to be seen, they are hard to remove when stuck in the skin: you would be wise to resist the temptation to touch *Opuntia* cacti.

The fruits of many species are juicy and edible, and sold in Mexican markets under the name of *tuna*. It is important to remember that fruits are covered with glochids, and must be peeled carefully before being eaten. *Nopalito* is the Mexican name given to young tender pads; these are cooked and eaten as a vegetable.

*Opuntia engelmannii*

var. *echinocarpa*

# 1·SILVER or GOLD CHOLLA

The sheaths of the silver or gold cholla come in two colors, white and yellow; hence the two different names. The plants are otherwise identical. This cholla is bushy with a definite short trunk and many short terminal branches at the ends of longer ones. The flowers are greenish-yellow. The fruits are spiny and dry up when ripe, rather than becoming fleshy as they do in many other chollas. This is a cactus of the dry desert of western Arizona and California.

*Opuntia echinocarpa* Engelmann & Bigelow
   Vars. *echinocarpa*
          *wolfii*
**Size:** up to 5 feet high
**Elevation:** 1,000–5,000 feet
**Distribution:** southeastern California, southern Nevada, western Arizona

# 2·DIAMOND CHOLLA

Growing in the drier parts of the western deserts, the diamond cholla is usually a low shrub not more than a couple of feet high. In some areas, such as Joshua Tree National Monument, the plants occasionally reach a height of 5 feet. Branches are the width of a thick pencil, grayish in color, and the surface is grooved, producing diamond-shaped tubercles. No other cholla has a grooved surface. The spines are usually one to an areole, quite long, and stand straight out from the body of the cactus. The spine sheaths are prominent, a light yellow or tan with a bright orange tip. When the sunlight is just right, the whole cactus glows, making this one of the more attractive chollas. The flowers are yellow to brownish-pink, and the fruits are dry and spiny, almost burr-like.

This cholla is found from Organ Pipe Cactus National Monument in the east to Southeastern California and Death Valley National Monument in the west. It grows best in sandy flat areas in the driest desert.

*Opuntia ramosissima* Engelmann
**Size:** 2 to 5 feet high
**Elevation:** 100–3,000 feet
**Distribution:** southeastern California, southern Nevada, and southwestern Arizona

# 3·BUCKHORN CHOLLA

This cholla is widespread from southern California to eastern Arizona. It is quite a variable species over this large territory. Tree-like in the western part of its range, it becomes shrubby in central and eastern Arizona. The branches of this cactus are rather long and straggly, giving the plant an open appearance. Spine sheaths of the buckhorn cholla are light in color, but are not prominent, allowing the color of the cactus body to show through. The normal color of the plant is light to dark green, but in time of drought or cold weather it often becomes reddish or purplish. The color change is a response of the plant to stress, and is found in many cacti. Because the spines are of different lengths and tend to cross over each other, the general appearance of this cholla is one of shagginess or unkemptness. One variety of this cholla has fewer and shorter spines, so that it looks almost spineless. The flowers are showy, and range from lemon-yellow to orange, pink, or red. The fruits are spiny and dry at maturity. The Pima Indians of Arizona are reputed to have steamed and eaten flower buds of this species.

*Opuntia acanthocarpa* Engelmann & Bigelow
    Vars. *acanthocarpa*
          *coloradensis*
          *ganderi*
          *major*
          *thornberi*
**Size:** 3 to 10 feet high
**Elevation:** 1,000–4,000 feet
**Distribution:** southeastern California, southern Nevada, southwestern Utah, and southern Arizona

var. *ganderi*

# 4·CHRISTMAS CHOLLA

The terminal joints of the Christmas cholla are often less than a quarter of an inch in diameter, making this cholla the most slender of its kind. Like the diamond cholla, it usually bears one long spine per areole, bent somewhat downward, and the showy sheaths are pale in color; but unlike that species, it has smooth branches, usually uninterrupted by any tubercles. The youngest branches are quite short, stand out at right angles, and are easily detached. The name Christmas cholla is given to this cactus because the fruits ripen to grape-size, red globes during the winter months. These bright red, occasionally yellow, juicy fruits stand out in the bleak winter vegetation, and are a favorite of birds. Sometimes the fruit will give rise to a green shoot, which in turn will flower, set fruit and may repeat the process again. This happens in some other species of chollas, but rarely with other cacti. This cholla is a sprawling shrub or on rare occasions vine-like. It grows best under the protection of other vegetation, and is thus not always noticed, but felt if one walks into it! The flowers of this species are greenish, yellow, or bronze in color. This is the most widespread of all the chollas; it is found throughout the southern half of Arizona, New Mexico, Texas, and even in part of Oklahoma.

*Opuntia leptocaulis* DeCandolle
**Size:** up to 4 feet high, rarely 6 feet or more
**Elevation:** 200–5,000 feet
**Distribution:** southern Arizona, southern New Mexico, Texas, south-central Oklahoma

# 5·CANE CHOLLA

As you travel up from the desert into the mountains you may be surprised to find the cane cholla still growing among the trees as it did lower in the desert. Clearly it has a high frost tolerance. This tall species is equally at home in the desert, grassland, or lower mountain slopes. The cane cholla develops a trunk or trunks and thick, tuberculate branches covered with grayish-colored spines. The spine sheaths are also gray but inconspicuous, and drop off early. At a short distance the cholla looks smooth and velvety due to the dense covering of the even, gray spines; this effect is peculiar to this cholla. The terminal branches stand out at a right angle but tend to droop. In the cold of winter the cactus usually turns purple. The normal flower color is a deep red-violet, but plants with yellow, orange, or even white flowers are not rare. The fruits of this species are fleshy, tuberculate, and spineless, turning lemon-yellow in winter. The combination of yellow fruits and purple joints is beautiful indeed.

When a cholla dies, the softer tissues quickly disintegrate, leaving a woody cylinder with more or less circular holes where the spine clusters used to be located. Each species of cholla has its own individual skeleton pattern. Since that of the cane cholla is particularly attractive, souvenirs such as canes and lamp bases are made from it.

*Opuntia spinosior* (Engelmann) Toumey
**Size:** up to 8 + feet high
**Elevation:** 2,000–6,500 + feet
**Distribution:** south-central to southeastern Arizona, southwestern New Mexico

# 6·TREE CHOLLA

When you see the tree cholla smothered under the snow of central Colorado, it is difficult to realize that this is the same cactus that grows in the desert of west Texas and northern Mexico. At a distance it looks something like the cane cholla, but with a closer look you see how much fatter are the branches and the tubercles. The spines are not proportionately larger, and thus are not as evident as in the cane cholla. The general effect is of a green, but not very spiny plant, which like the cane cholla becomes purplish in cold weather. It also bears large yellow, tuberculate fruits. Flowers are usually deep rose-violet.

*Opuntia imbricata* (Haworth) DeCandolle
**Size:** up to 8 + feet high
**Elevation:** 2,000–6,000 + feet
**Distribution:** central and eastern Colorado, New Mexico, western and central Texas, western Kansas, western Oklahoma

# 7·STAGHORN CHOLLA

This medium to tall, tree-like cactus has an open crown, and wand-like terminal branches. Although these dull green branches are only slightly more slender than those of the cane and buckhorn chollas, their great length gives an impression of thinness. The spines are short and the sheaths inconspicuous: the joints give a feeling of neatness. Typical plants of the buckhorn, cane, and staghorn chollas are distinct enough that they can be told apart. Unfortunately these species tend to hybridize where their ranges overlap, so if you experience difficulties identifying one of these chollas, you may have come across one of these hybrids.

This cholla takes its species name, *versicolor*, from the great variability of the color of its flowers. The fruits are spineless, smooth and never turn bright yellow. They are often proliferous, and short fruit chains are not unusual. The range of this cactus is restricted to an area that does not extend much more than about 80 miles around Tucson, Arizona, but it is common in Sonora, Mexico.

*Opuntia versicolor* Engelmann
**Size:** 3 to 15 feet high
**Elevation:** 2,000–3,000 feet
**Distribution:** Pinal county and eastern Pima counties, Arizona

# 8·JUMPING or CHAINFRUIT CHOLLA

This cholla is a dweller of the flat desert, where it may form veritable forests. In youth it is symmetrical and looks attractive with its long spines covered with straw-colored sheaths that shine in the desert sunlight. Later, the trunk or trunks supporting long branches turn black, while the short branches at the top of the plant hang down every which way. This cholla can grow up to 15 feet in height, although most plants are shorter. The primary way the jumping cholla reproduces is to drop its short terminal joints on the ground where they take root and form new plants. Do not walk close to this cholla; you are sure to pick up one of these joints on your shoe or leg. Once imbedded, the barbed spines are extremely difficult to pull out. The joints attach themselves so easily to whomever brushes against them that they seem to "jump" at you; they do not, of course. The flowers are violet and the fruits green and proliferous to the extent that long chains of fruits are very common, hence the name chainfruit cholla. These fruits are usually sterile.

Another form of this cholla is often encountered growing together with the normal form. It is shorter, and the spines are poorly developed; the plant looks quite green instead of straw-colored. Although it looks like a different species altogether, it is just a genetic variant.

*Opuntia fulgida* Engelmann
**Size:** to 15 feet high
**Elevation:** 1,000–3,000 feet
**Distribution:** southern Arizona

# 9·TEDDY BEAR CHOLLA

This cholla may look as cuddly as a teddy bear, but do not caress it! Its long spines are strongly barbed, and the joints of the cactus will readily come off the plant and become imbedded in whomever brushes against them. Pliers may be needed to pull out the spines. This treacherous cactus prefers sunny, rocky slopes in the hot desert. Although it has attractive greenish-white flowers in the spring, it relies almost completely on dropped joints for reproduction. These root easily where they land. Pack rats that live in the desert where the teddy bear cholla grows carry off fallen joints to cover their nests as camouflage and protection. The dense covering of golden sheathed spines makes this one of the most handsome members of the desert community. With its short compact branches, this cactus is less sprawling than most other species of chollas.

*Opuntia bigelovii* Engelmann
**Size:** 4 to 12 feet high
**Elevation:** 100–3,500 feet
**Distribution:** southern California, extreme southern Nevada, northwestern and southern Arizona east to Tucson

# 10·PENCIL CHOLLA

The branches of this cactus are not as thin as a pencil, but more the size of a thick fountain pen. They are deep green and rarely have tubercles, except when shrivelled due to a long dry spell. One long spine is the usual number per areole. There is a definite short, thick trunk topped by a profusion of short joints. The overall effect is that of a compact green mass. This is not one of the chollas that turns red or purple in winter. It bears yellow to orange flowers, and its fruits are fleshy and greenish. The only other chollas with which it could be confused are the Christmas and Klein's chollas, but both of these are sprawling and trunkless, and the Christmas cholla has much thinner branches and bright red fruits.

The pencil cholla is not distributed evenly over its range, but instead occurs in disjunct populations of many individual plants. It prefers level ground where the soil is not too shallow.

*Opuntia arbuscula* Engelmann
**Size:** 2 to 4 + feet high
**Elevation:** 1,000–4,200 feet
**Distribution:** southern Arizona

# 11·KLEIN'S CHOLLA

This sprawling open-crowned cholla with prominent sheathed spines is found from west Texas, where it forms large thickets, to southern Arizona and New Mexico where it occurs in small isolated groups or as individual plants greatly distant from one another, and thus hard to find. A good place to see it in Arizona is at the lower elevations of Saguaro National Monument West, where it grows with the pencil cholla. In west Texas it is prominent in the Davis Mountains and parts of the Big Bend country. The spines usually are four to a cluster and are pointed down; the joints have prominent tubercles and the cactus is practically trunkless. The flowers are pinkish to violet, and the fruits are orange to reddish and smooth.

Although it has the same general habit of growth as the Christmas cholla, it can be told apart from that species by its much thicker, tuberculate branches, and its fruits, which are not bright red, but varying degrees of orange and red.

*Opuntia kleiniae* DeCandolle
**Size:** 3 to 6 + feet high
**Elevation:** 2,000–6,000 + feet
**Distribution:** Arizona, New Mexico, west Texas

var. *stanlyi*

# 12 · DEVIL CHOLLA

The devil cholla is in a different group of cacti called club chollas. The name comes from the shape of the joints, which are club-shaped with well defined tubercles. These are low growing cacti that often form mats along the ground. Branching occurs mostly at the base of older joints with the newly formed branches lying along the ground. Club chollas have no sheaths on their spines which are usually flattened and dagger-like and quite capable of piercing shoe leather or finger nails. These spines may be pink, yellow, brown or red in youth, but usually turn chalky white or gray. Since the spines form a dense network, the plants also look gray, at least at a distance. The devil cholla · sometimes covers large patches of ground in the desert or grassland, making it virtually impossible for man or horse to pass through. In central New Mexico, where it grows in grasslands, it may resemble clumps of dried grass in the distance. The flowers of these cacti are lemon-yellow. Different species and varieties grow from southern California across Arizona and New Mexico and into Texas. These may vary somewhat, but all are recognizable as forms of this cholla and have all been included under the name of devil cholla.

*Opuntia stanlyi* Engelmann
  Vars. *stanlyi*
    *kunzei*
    *parishii*
**Size:** to 12 inches high
**Elevation:** 300–4,000 feet
**Distribution:** southern California to southwestern New Mexico

*Opuntia schottii* Engelmann
**Size:** plant to 4 inches high
**Elevation:** 1,000–5,000 feet
**Distribution:** west Texas

*Opuntia clavata* Engelmann
**Size:** plant to 4 inches high
**Elevation:** 6,000–8,000 feet
**Distribution:** central New Mexico

var. *kunzei*

# 13 · PLAINS PRICKLY PEAR

You may not realize that cacti grow as far north as Canada. The plains prickly pear is one of these hardy plants. In fact it is one of the most widespread of all cacti. It occurs as far south as west Texas, and another form of it grows in southern California. This is one of the diminutive prickly pears that hugs the ground. The pads are small, rarely as much as 5 inches long, and the spine clusters are crowded together. The forms of this cactus that grow in the Southwest are quite spiny. Some of these bear short thick spines, while the spines of others are long and hair-like. Flowers are yellow, less often pink. This and the beavertail are the only prickly pears in the Southwest that have dry fruits at maturity. The pads often become wrinkled with the coming of winter, due to a loss of water in the cells of the plant. This is a means of increasing frost resistance by concentrating the cell sap. It is the plants equivalent of putting antifreeze in the car's radiator.

*Opuntia polyacantha*

*Opuntia polyacantha* Haworth
**Size:** 1 foot high or less
**Elevation:** 4,000–10,000 feet
**Distribution:** southern California, southern Nevada, New Mexico, west Texas

*Opuntia erinacea* Engelmann & Bigelow
**Size:** 1 foot high or less
**Elevation:** 1,500–7,500 feet
**Distribution:** southern California, southern Nevada

*Opuntia erinacea*

# 14 · BEAVERTAIL

The beavertail is one of the prickly pears that is easy to recognize. The shape of its pads (like a beaver's tail), its lack of spines and its blue-gray color give it away. It branches from the lower parts of the older pads and thus remains low to the ground, seldom more than two pads high. One unusual feature of this and the blind pear is that the surface of the pads is covered with fine hairs; you can pass your finger over the cactus and feel the velvety texture (being careful to stay away from the areoles filled with glochids!). The flowers of this very attractive cactus are a deep rose color, and the fruits are dry at maturity.

*Opuntia basilaris* Engelmann & Bigelow
**Size:** about 1 foot high
**Elevation:** sea level–9,000 feet
**Distribution:** southern California, southern Nevada, western Arizona, southwestern Utah

# 15 · BLIND PEAR

One other spineless prickly pear of the Southwest is the blind pear of the Big Bend. It is really a Mexican species that crosses the border only in the Big Bend region of Texas. Unlike the beavertail, it is a tall plant with large pads about 6 inches in diameter; these are usually circular or sometimes a little elongated. Their color is gray-green to yellow-green, the latter color being more pronounced in times of drought. The pads of this species are also covered with fine hairs and have a velvety feel. The many clusters of reddish glochids are a striking feature of the plant. In this species the glochids are very loosely attached and will blow away in a strong wind, or if the plant is shaken. Cattle have been blinded by these blowing glochids, which is why the name "blind pear" was applied to this cactus by cattlemen. The flowers are bright yellow when they first open, but turn orange with age. The fruits are fleshy and red.

*Opuntia rufida* Engelmann
**Size:** up to 6 feet high
**Elevation:** 2,000–3,500 feet
**Distribution:** Big Bend Region of Texas

# 16 · TUBEROUS PRICKLY PEAR

The tuberous prickly pear is one more species that grows low to the ground. Like the plains prickly pear, it is a very diminutive plant whose small pads become wrinkled with the coming of winter. But unlike that prickly pear it has juicy fruits and few spines, which are found only in the upper parts of the pad. The surface of the pads is most often dark green, but is sometimes bluish-green. It was given the scientific name *macrorhiza*, meaning "large root," because the first plants discovered were found to have tuberous roots in addition to the ordinary fibrous ones. Actually, not all plants of this species have tuberous roots. The flowers are yellow with red centers, or sometimes all red. This is not usually a plant of the desert, but rather of the prairies, and in the Southwest is also found in the mountains.

*Opuntia macrorhiza* Engelmann
**Size:** up to 6 inches high
**Elevation:** 2,000–9,000 feet
**Distribution:** central and eastern Arizona, east to the Mississippi River

# 17 · BROWN-SPINED PRICKLY PEAR

A common cactus of the desert, the brown-spined prickly pear is a medium high, trunkless shrub that sometimes forms clumps many feet in diameter. The pale bluish-green, oblong pads (4 to 6 inches long) grow upright in this species and often root on contact with the soil. Thus as one pad grows from the previous one, they form short chains along the ground. The spines are somewhat flattened, reddish-brown, and are most conspicuous in the upper parts of the pads. Its spine clusters are far apart. The flowers are yellow, sometimes reddish at their bases. The fruits are plump and juicy, red to purple in color.

Like most prickly pears, this species needs well-drained soil of a coarse nature. For this reason it is rarely found growing in the lower parts of desert valleys where soils are usually heavy. Although plentiful in the desert, this cactus is also found in montane environments.

*Opuntia phaeacantha* Engelmann
　Vars. *phaeacantha*
　　　*major*
**Size:** 2 to 3 feet high
**Elevation:** 2,000–8,000 feet
**Distribution:** southern California, Arizona, New Mexico, Texas, Colorado, Utah

var. *major*

# 18·PURPLE PRICKLY PEAR

Botanists are not agreed as to whether the purple and the Santa Rita prickly pears are different forms of the same species. Because of their dissimilar appearance, I have treated them as different entities. The pads of this cactus are oblong, with long black (sometimes white) needle-like spines that stick out of the upper parts of the pads. The color of the cactus is bluish to purple, as in the Santa Rita prickly pear, but the purple prickly pear is a shorter plant. The flowers are yellow with red centers, making this prickly pear an attractive member of the desert community.

The Santa Rita prickly pear is common in eastern Arizona, and relatively uncommon in west Texas. The purple prickly pear is very plentiful in west Texas and poorly represented in eastern Arizona.

*Opuntia violacea* Engelmann
   var. *macrocentra* (Engelmann) L. Benson
**Size:** to 3 + feet high
**Elevation:** 3,000–5,500 feet
**Distribution:** southeastern Arizona, southwestern New Mexico, west Texas

var. *macrocentra*

var. *santa-rita*

# *19* · SANTA RITA PRICKLY PEAR

The bluish to purple color of this cactus makes the desert south of Tucson especially colorful. Normally there are no spines on this prickly pear, but an occasional reddish-brown needle-like spine may form near the top of the nearly circular pads. The Santa Rita prickly pear is a fairly tall cactus that usually does not have a trunk. The purplish coloration, due to the pigment betacyanin, is produced by the plant as a response to either cold or lack of available water. Even more striking is the deep maroon of the developing pads. The combination of lavender pads and lemon-yellow flowers is striking. The Santa Rita prickly pear and the blind pear resemble each other, but the former is never hairy, and the latter never turns purple.

*Opuntia violacea* Engelmann
var. *santa-rita* (Griffiths & Hare)
L. Benson
**Size:** up to 6 feet high
**Elevation:** 3,000–5,000 feet
**Distribution:** southeastern Arizona, southwestern New Mexico, west Texas

var. *santa-rita*

# 20·ENGELMANN'S PRICKLY PEAR

This, another common cactus of the Southwest, and one of the most massive, has the largest pads (up to 12 inches long) of any native prickly pear in the United States. It forms large trunkless mounds many feet across and up to 5 feet tall, with blue-green circular or oblong pads. Characteristic of this species are the widely spaced clusters of white, flattened, down-pointing spines. Flowers are yellow, followed by large fruits that are purplish-red and juicy. It is found on lower mountain slopes as well as on the desert floor.

*Opuntia engelmannii* Salm-Dyck Ex. Engelmann
**Size:** up to 5 feet high
**Elevation:** 1,500–6,200 feet
**Distribution:** southern California, western to southeastern Arizona, southern New Mexico, west Texas

---

# 21·TEXAS PRICKLY PEAR

This is another tall prickly pear whose pads are almost as large as those of Engelmann's. These two prickly pears are very similar to one another and are considered by some botanists to represent two varieties of the same species. The Texas prickly pear has needle-like, translucent yellow spines while those of Engelmann's prickly pear are flattened and chalky white. This may be the best way to tell these two cacti apart. The Texas prickly pear is principally a plant of eastern and central Texas, but it does reach west Texas and extreme southeastern New Mexico. It can also be seen along the Rio Grande in the Big Bend area of Texas.

*Opuntia lindheimeri* Engelmann
**Size:** up to 5 + feet high
**Elevation:** sea level–4,600 feet
**Distribution:** southeastern New Mexico, west Texas to Gulf of Mexico

# 22·PANCAKE PRICKLY PEAR

If many prickly pears are trunkless, this species makes up for them. Its circular pads arise from the thick, round trunk to form a plant that is wider at the top, somewhat in the shape of a three dimensional "Y." The pads are bluish, with crowded clusters of thin, pale yellow spines, most of which point down. As this cactus ages, the areoles along the trunk and older pads develop many more spines, so that the cactus often assumes a shaggy look and a hairy silhouette. Petals are yellow with reddish centers while the fruits are fleshy and gray with purplish overtones. With one exception, this prickly pear is restricted to rocky ledges and steep rock slopes on mountain foothills or at higher elevations. Although there is no explanation, one population of this cactus inhabits flat places in the desert in the vicinity of Aguila in western Arizona. In this region, the plants reach much larger sizes than elsewhere.

*Opuntia chlorotica* Engelmann & Bigelow
**Size:** up to 7 feet high
**Elevation:** 2,000–6,000 feet
**Distribution:** southern California, southern Nevada, western to southeastern Arizona, southwestern New Mexico

# 23·BEARDED PRICKLY PEAR

This small, upright, trunkless prickly pear has a very restricted range, being found in a limited area just east of the Big Bend of Texas. There it occurs only on limestone ridges. It is striking in appearance due to its brightly colored spines. These are short, point down and are brown at their bases, red in the middle, and yellow at their tips. They contrast handsomely with the yellow-green of the small oblong pads. Like the pancake prickly pear, this cactus has a shaggy appearance. The flowers are cream-colored and the fruits bright red and very small.

*Opuntia strigil* Engelmann
**Size:** 2 to 3 feet high
**Elevation:** 3,000–4,500 feet
**Distribution:** Crockett, Pecos, and Terrell Counties, Texas

---

# 24·SPINY-FRUITED PRICKLY PEAR

It was only thirty years ago that this cactus was discovered in Big Bend National Park. Since it forms such a small population there, and has not been found anywhere else, it is believed to be of hybrid origin. This species has a short trunk and upright pads, which are elongated and yellow-green with heavy, orange to brown spines spreading in all directions. The areoles are raised on mounds, a condition not normally found in prickly pears. The flowers are yellow-orange with red bases. The fruits are fleshy, yellow-green, and spiny, which is most unusual for fleshy fruited prickly pears.

*Opuntia spinosibacca* Anthony
**Size:** up to 4 feet high
**Elevation:** 2,000–3,000 feet
**Distribution:** Big Bend National Park, Texas

# CEREUS

This very large group of cacti is widespread throughout the Americas, especially near the tropics, in regions where the climate is dry. Relatively few cerei are natives of the United States, but many exotic species are cultivated outdoors where temperatures are mild.

Many cerei are tree-like and extremely massive, while others are bushy or even vine-like. Whatever their habits of growth, they are always ribbed, and long relative to their girth.

Flowers of this group arise in the upper part of the spine-bearing areoles.

Many, perhaps most, of the species have night blooming flowers. Since flower color (whose purpose is to attract pollinators) is not visible at night, nocturnal blossoms tend to be white or pale colored. On the other hand night fragrances attract pollinators and these blooms are often strongly perfumed.

GEORGE H.H. HUEY

*Stenocereus thurberi*

# 25·SAGUARO

GEORGE H.H. HUEY

The monarch of the desert is one of the largest cacti anywhere; perhaps it is the tallest. Although the saguaro usually does not grow taller than 40 feet, some plants have been measured at more than 50 feet. Early in its life, as a tiny plant, it needs the protection of other vegetation to survive under the harsh conditions of the desert. The saguaro grows many years as an unbranched tree with a ribbed surface. This fluting allows the cactus to expand or contract like an accordion as its roots absorb water from the ground, or as it becomes dessicated. Many cacti are ribbed, which seems to be an adaptive response to water availability.

After a great many years, saguaros may branch; most commonly all branches arise from one level on the plant, high above the ground. Occasionally, additional branches form even higher up. The saguaro, when young, produces heavy, thick, dark spines. As it becomes old enough to flower, around fifty years of age, the spines formed on new growth are thin, almost bristle-like, and light in color. This modification of spine form in age is not unusual in tall species of cacti.

During the month of May, the white waxy flowers form near the tip of each branch and of the main trunk. These open toward evening, stay open much of the next day, and then close not to reopen again. A few weeks later the green fruits ripen and burst open, revealing the bright red juicy pulp, which from a distance looks like a red flower; indeed many people have assumed that this cactus has red flowers! The tasty pulp of the fruit has always been an important part of the Tohono O'odham (Papago) Indians' diet. The pulp may be eaten as is, made into jelly, or fermented into wine. The seeds, which are abundant and rich in oil, are ground and also eaten.

Upper parts of the trunk and branches of the saguaro are in great demand for nest sites by woodpeckers who hollow out chambers. Later on, when the woodpeckers abandon their nests, tiny elf owls or other birds move in.

Since seeds of this cactus need summer rains to germinate this excludes it from southern California (except along parts of the Colorado River), where rains normally fall only during the winter months. Saguaros can endure frosts for short periods of time; where these last longer than about 24 hours, they cannot survive. At the northern edge of their range, they grow on south facing hillsides where morning sunlight quickly raises the ambient temperature above freezing. In warmer areas they will grow on level ground, but they need a rocky substratum for good anchorage. Saguaros growing on deep alluvial soils that become soft after a heavy rain are subject to toppling over in high winds.

*Carnegiea gigantea* (Engelmann) Britton & Rose
**Size:** to 50 + feet high
**Elevation:** 600–nearly 5,000 feet
**Distribution:** western and south central Arizona to a little east of Tucson

# 26·ORGAN PIPE CACTUS

The appearance of the organ pipe cactus is quite different from that of the saguaro as it has no central stem. Instead, it has many relatively slender branches that arise from a central point at ground level, and then curve upward gracefully. In fact, it is a tidy looking plant. Under optimum conditions, branching occurs only at or near the base of older branches. In the northern part of its range, where frosts occur regularly, the tips of the newest branches often freeze and die. The next growing season the plant will grow new branches from just below the dead tips. Plants in Arizona are branched at all levels, while further south in Mexico, where there is no frost, little branching occurs above ground level. Branches have many deep green, rounded ribs. The felt of their areoles is dark red, and the spines are dark or gray. Flowers are smaller than those of the saguaro and are white to pale lavender. The developing fruits are spiny, lose their spines at maturity and then open up, showing the edible red pulp. The local Indians make use of this tasty fruit in much the same way as they do with those of the saguaro. This cactus is widespread in western Mexico, but in the United States it is found only in Organ Pipe Cactus National Monument and sporadically further west and north. It favors south facing hillsides, but also grows on level ground. Like the saguaro, it does not like heavy alluvial soils.

*Stenocereus thurberi* (Engelmann) Buxbaum
**Size:** up to 20 feet high
**Elevation:** 1,000–3,500 feet
**Distribution:** Organ Pipe Cactus National Monument and vicinity, Arizona

Like the organ pipe, this species branches from the base, but its ribs are few, sharp-angled and light-green. While the organ pipe gives an impression of neatness, the senita look dishevelled. There are many long and short branches, several of which arch over, and an ever present number of dead limbs. When an individual of this species is young, its spines are short, heavy and few per cluster. As the plant becomes older, it begins to produce spines of a different character—these are long, bristly and very numerous. Thus the ends of the tallest branches, which are the youngest in age, are gray and bristly. This gives the impression that the cactus is white-haired like an old man. In old age these long spines turn black. It is only in the region of bristles that flowering takes place. The flowers are small and light pink; more than one forms at an areole, a phenomenon rare in the cactus family. The fruits are red outside and inside, and spineless.

Within its range, it favors flat sandy ground. In Mexico, where it is more common, it forms part of the popular medicine: decoctions made from the stems have been used in the treatment of cancer and diabetes.

*Lophocereus schottii* (Engelmann) Britton & Rose
**Size:** up to 20 feet high
**Elevation:** 1,500 feet
**Distribution:** Organ Pipe Cactus National Monument, Arizona

# 28·QUEEN OF THE NIGHT

This is one of the strangest looking cacti, and so inconspicuous it is rarely seen in the wild unless by chance. It needs the shade of desert shrubs (most often creosote bush) where it is found, well hidden and looking much like the dead branches of the plants under whose protection it grows. Even a few feet away, the plant is hard to recognize. Very close by, the dead sticks resolve themselves into half-inch-thick stems whose surface is gray with a slight bluish tinge and covered with a fine velvet. The spines along the four to six ribs are plentiful but extremely small and not very conspicuous. The branches may grow to be several feet long if supported by the nurse plant, but usually are shorter. Being woody they break off easily, sometimes even to the ground. This does not cause any serious problems for this most unusual cactus because most of its reserves of food and water are underground: the root is enormous and turnip-shaped, weighing up to a hundred pounds or more. With this reserve of energy new stems will soon sprout. This root is edible and has been a source of food for local Indians. They also used the root as a poultice for respiratory ills.

The real splendor of this plant does not become apparent until it flowers in mid-June. The blooms are large (8 inches long) and trumpet-shaped, with showy white petals and stamens. They open as night falls, diffusing an exquisite fragrance. These delicate jewels close with the first rays of the rising sun and do not reopen again. The flowers are followed by fruits that are large, bright red, and edible.

*Peniocereus greggii* (Engelmann) Britton & Rose
**Size:** branches are up to 10 feet long, ½ inch thick
**Elevation:** 1,000–5,000 feet
**Distribution:** southern Arizona, southwestern New Mexico, west Texas

# ECHINOCEREUS
## (*Hedgehog Cacti*)

    Hedgehog cacti include a large number of highly variable species in the genus *Echinocereus*. Some hedgehogs are long-spined, but many are not; they are relatively short-stemmed and always ribbed. Some species are single-stemmed while others branch to an extraordinary extent from the base to form large mounds. Their usually showy flowers make these plants especially attractive . Instead of forming in the areoles as they do in other cacti, the flower buds develop just above the areoles, but underneath the surface of the rib and then burst through the tissues. The flowers are usually borne in the upper parts of the stems but in some species they also occur lower down. Fruits are all edible, and some are delicious. These are covered with spines, which become loose at maturity and can be brushed off. Most hedgehogs like full sun.

*Echinocereus reichenbachii*

var. *neo-mexicanus*

# 29 · CLARET CUP

This, the most widespread of all hedge-hog species, is also the most variable in appearance. The several varieties of this cactus are so different looking that it is hard to believe that they are members of a single species. What unites them is their nearly identical flowers. These are bright red with rounded petal tips. No other hedgehog has red flowers in this country, and most others have pointed petals. The fruits are red, juicy, and edible.

These cacti often form large rounded mounds composed of as many as five hundred stems tightly packed together. Spines are at first yellow, pink, or sometimes nearly black, turning whitish-gray after their first season. The plants then look pale colored in very spiny varieties. Forms with few spines always look green. In variety *mojavensis* (of southern California and Nevada), the spines are conspicuously twisted.

Although some claret cups are found in the desert in west Texas and southern California, this hedgehog occurs mainly in the uplands and mountains bordering the desert.

*Echinocereus triglochidiatus* Engelmann
Vars. *triglochidiatus*
  *arizonicus*
  *gurneyi*
  *melanacanthus*
  *mojavensis*
  *neo-mexicanus*
  *paucispinus*
**Size:** 4 to 12 inches high
**Elevation:** 1,500–10,000 feet
**Distribution:** Southern California, southern Nevada to west Texas

var. *gurneyi*

## 30 · LEDING'S HEDGEHOG

If you drive up the Mount Graham Highway in the Pinaleno Mountains of southeastern Arizona, you will be able to see the yellow clusters of Leding's hedgehog which cling to the rocky outcrops. The tight clusters consist of a few to many cylindrical stems. The spines which are uniformally luminous pale-yellow, only partially hide the light green color of the stems. The main central spines are thick and much longer than any of the other spines; they point down and give this hedgehog its characteristic appearance.

The large flowers are deep violet and the fruits greenish to reddish.

Although reported from many of the southeastern Arizona peaks, the Pinaleno Mountains is the only place you are likely to see this species.

*Echinocereus ledingii* Peebles
**Size:** to 20 inches high
**Elevation:** 4,000–6,600 + feet
**Distribution:** Southeastern Arizona in the mountains, but primarily in the Pinaleno Mountains, Graham County

## 31 · FENDLER'S HEDGEHOG

This is another cactus that grows above the desert proper. It is found in grassland and among oaks, junipers, and pinyon pines. It has beautiful, large magenta flowers that makes it stand out from its surroundings. This hedgehog does not form mounds. In the northern part of its range stems are often solitary, but in southern Arizona it is a somewhat larger and taller plant consisting of up to five stems whose ribs are almost broken up into tubercles. Spines are few and not very long, thus allowing the green color of the plant to show plainly. There is one dark central spine, which points outward; the radials are white for the most part, although there are always a few streaked with brown or black. The edible fruits are purplish.

*Echinocereus fendleri* Engelmann
    Vars. *fendleri*
        *rectispinus*
**Size:** up to 10 inches high
**Elevation:** 3,000–8,000 feet
**Distribution:** northeastern and southeastern Arizona, western New Mexico

var. *rectispinus*

var. *fasciculatus*

# 32·ROBUST HEDGEHOG

This is the only hedgehog common in the vicinity of Tucson. As the name implies, it is a robust looking cactus whose tall stems form small clumps. Its long spines are numerous and of uneven length, thus giving the plants a shaggy appearance. They are dense enough to obscure the surface of the stems. Spines are yellow, orange, brown, white, or even black; all of these colors sometimes can be found on the same plant.

Flowers are large, showy and variable in color, but always consisting of some shade of violet or magenta. You may even come across a plant with nearly white flowers. The fruits are purplish and very tasty.

There are two other varieties of this hedgehog that are more restricted in their distribution. Variety *bonkerae* inhabits high elevations. Because of its extremely short spines, it appears smoother and smaller than the others. Variety *boyce-thompsonii* has long, slender spines that are almost bristle-like. Both varieties have more numerous ribs: up to eighteen instead of about ten.

*Echinocereus fasciculatus* (Engelmann) L. Benson
   Vars. *fasciculatus*
       *bonkerae*
       *boyce-thompsonii*
**Size:** to 12 + inches high
**Elevation:** 1,000–6,000 feet
**Distribution:** south-central to extreme southwestern New Mexico

var. *boyce-thompsonii*

# 33·ENGELMANN'S HEDGEHOG

Here is another species of hedgehog cactus that is subdivided into several varieties that are hard to tell apart. As a matter of fact it is sometimes difficult to distinguish this species from the robust hedgehog. That cactus has one or two central spines that are round in cross-section, while the central spines of Engelmann's hedgehog are several in number, one or more of these flattened and sword-like. In general, Engelmann's hedgehog is a heavier, larger plant with stouter spines. The far western plants of this species have the thickest stems. The flowers of this hedgehog are much like those of the robust hedgehog, and so are the fruits. This cactus is definitely a plant of the desert, rarely occurring elsewhere. It is especially well represented in California and western Arizona.

One variety of Engelmann's hedgehog stands out as distinct enough to be mentioned here. This is variety *nicholii* whose stems are extremely long, golden spined, form large clusters, and whose flowers are much paler in color; it is common in Organ Pipe Cactus National Monument.

*Echinocereus engelmannii* (Parry) Lemaire
Vars. *engelmannii*
 *acicularis*
 *armatus*
 *chrysocentrus*
 *nicholii*
**Size:** to 13 inches high (24 inches in var. *nicholii*)
**Elevation:** 1,000–5,000 feet
**Distribution:** southern California, southern Nevada to south-central Arizona

var. *nicholii*

# 34·GREEN STRAWBERRY HEDGEHOG

This cactus is easily recognized by its long, flabby, bright green stems that tend to lie flat on the ground with only their upper parts upright. The plants look green because the spines, although long, are few per cluster, and also because the areoles are far apart. The plants, often growing under shrubs, consist of sprawling clusters with many stems. Flowers are large, showy, and magenta in color. Fruits are greenish-brown, said to taste like strawberries, and therefore much sought after. This hedgehog is found along the entire length of the Rio Grande in Texas.

*Echinocereus enneacanthus* Engelmann
**Size:** up to 12 + inches long
**Elevation:** sea level–3,000 feet
**Distribution:** Texas, along the Rio Grande

# 35·SPINY STRAWBERRY HEDGEHOG

This hedgehog is a mound builder; some of the mounds can be as much as 5 feet across and are reminiscent of the mounds formed by claret cups. On spiny strawberry hedgehogs, however, the spines, which are very long and straw-colored, often obliterate the outline of the individual stems, so that the mounds look like heaps of straw. At flowering time they become covered with large, deep pinkish-red blooms. The fruits are reddish-purple and also have a delicious strawberry flavor. This cactus is quite common along the limestone hills of west Texas, which in some places are actually covered with the straw-colored mounds.

*Echinocereus stramineus* (Engelmann) Rümpler
**Size:** stems up to 10 inches long
**Elevation:** 2,000–5,000 feet
**Distribution:** southeastern New Mexico, west Texas

Whereas other hedgehog cacti are protected by long heavy spines, the Arizona rainbow is enclosed in a veritable lattice of tiny spines that hides its body almost completely from the outside world. Certainly the effect of this heavy armament is to shade the plant from the sun's burning rays. The areoles of this cactus are crowded along the stem and the spines are short and close together. Each spine cluster looks like a pair of combs. These clusters lie flat along the curvature of the stem so that you may grasp the plant in your hand without fear of being pricked.

New growth in any cactus occurs at the top of the plant. Thus any circle of spines around the stem represents spines of the same age. In the rainbow hedgehog, successive circles of spines may be different colors, from white to cream, pink or even red. Thus the cactus seems to be made up of alternating color bands: hence the name "rainbow." Not every plant is so variegated and you may even come across some plants that are all white or all red. This cactus is roughly the shape of a fat cylinder and is usually unbranched.

Even when not flowering it is a most attractive plant, but when it flowers it is truly breathtaking. The blooms may be 4 inches across and are deep pink with a white center. The Arizona rainbow is found in grassland and oak woodland, where it does best on a substratum of granite or similar rocks.

*Echinocereus rigidissimus* (Engelmann) Rose
**Size:** to 12 inches high
**Elevation:** 4,000–5,500 + feet
**Distribution:** southeastern Arizona, extreme southwestern New Mexico

# 37·TEXAS RAINBOW

The Texas rainbow is a more slender plant than the Arizona rainbow. It has a rough appearance like a bottle brush because its clusters of tiny spines, instead of lying flat on the stem, stick out in all directions. This rainbow cactus is usually single-stemmed, but plants with branches are not uncommon. Spines may be variously straw-colored, yellow, orange or deep rust, but whatever their color, they hide the stem's surface quite effectively. Flowers are lemon-yellow with a green throat, although there are plants with orange, peach, or pink flowers. This is a common cactus of the Chihuahuan Desert and the nearby grasslands.

*Echinocereus pectinatus* (Scheidweiler) Engelmann
   Var. *neo-mexicanus* (Coulter) L. Benson
**Size:** to 14 inches high
**Elevation:** 4,000–5,000 feet
**Distribution:** southwestern New Mexico, west Texas

# 38·LACE CACTUS

Plants of this species are generally smaller in stature, and have finer spines than those of the other rainbows. Like many of the rainbows, the radial spines lie flat along the stems. The ovaries of the flowers are covered with very fine spines and long, white wooly hairs unlike those of the other described rainbows that have stout spines and almost no hairs. Flowers are also smaller, pale to deep pink, and particularly beautiful due to the satiny sheen of the petals which makes them glow in sunlight. In no other hedge-hog flower is this trait so pronounced. Within our area, this little jewel is only found in eastern New Mexico and extreme west Texas. It has always been a favorite of cactus fanciers, and many plants have been dug up to satisfy their demands.

*Echinocereus reichenbachii* (Terscheck) Haage f. ex. Britton & Rose
**Size:** up to 6 inches high
**Elevation:** 2,000–4,000 feet
**Distribution:** southeastern Colorado, eastern New Mexico, Oklahoma, central and western Texas

*var. viridiflorus*

# 39 · GREEN-FLOWERED RAINBOW

This little rainbow hedgehog, one of the hardiest species of cacti, is found from South Dakota to Mexico. Unlike other rainbows that have large showy flowers, this one has small blooms that may appear anywhere along the stem. Flower color is highly variable, ranging from greenish-yellow to orange or rust, or occasionally pinkish.

The green-flowered rainbow grows in grassy places as well as in true desert areas. The varieties common in southern New Mexico and west Texas differ from each other primarily in the length and number of spines in each cluster, but they are difficult to tell apart.

*Echinocereus viridiflorus* Engelmann
    Vars. *viridiflorus*
          *chloranthus*
          *russanthus*
**Size:** 3 to 10 inches high
**Elevation:** 2,300–5,400 feet
**Distribution:** southern New Mexico, west Texas

# FEROCACTUS & ECHINOCACTUS
## (*Barrels*)

Some large plants in this group are barrel-shaped. I do not know whether their common name stems from that fact or from the belief that if one of these cacti is cut open, refreshing water will run out to quench the thirst of the desert traveler. It is indeed possible, but difficult, to decapitate a barrel cactus and mash down the soft tissues so that a thick, unappetizing, but drinkable liquid is obtained. The quality of this liquid reportedly varies from mouth puckering to insipid. Certainly the taste would depend on the species of barrel and the condition of the plant.

Not all barrel cacti are large; some can be quite small. All members of this group have prominent ribs, and are all densely armed with heavy spines. In many species one or more central spines is recurved like a fishhook; to be sure, in the past Indians have used them for fishing.

Unlike those of hedgehogs, barrel flowers are always found at the top of the plant, very close to the growing point. The flowers and fruits bear no spines, only a few scales. The fruits become fleshy at maturity and some even juicy, but most of them are not considered edible.

*Ferocactus wislizenii*

# 40·ARIZONA BARREL

Although this barrel may reach a height of 8 feet or more, you are not likely to see one that size. Where it grows together with the saguaro, it might be mistaken for that species, but the saguaro is slender while the Arizona barrel is fat, barrel-shaped, and has stout hooked spines. This barrel often leans toward the southwest and occasionally will lean so far that it falls over. Young plants of all tall species of barrel cactus start out being globe shaped, and only begin to elongate when their diameter has become greater than about a foot. At this juvenile stage the spines are stouter and longer than those of mature plants. These young plants are particularly attractive.

The main central spine of this species is especially long, wide, flattened, crossed with little ridges and terminating in a down-pointing hook. Central spines are dark red beneath a gray surface layer. This red coloration comes through best when the spines are wet. In addition to its central spines, the Arizona barrel has a large number of white, bristle-like radial spines.

Flowers appear in August or September, much later than most cacti. They are orange-red and occasionally yellow. These are followed by fleshly, bright lemon-yellow fruits that stand out strikingly from the green of the stem. These fruits are a favorite of many animals and so do not last long. The fruits and the interior of the stems of this and other barrels have been used to make cactus candy. This has led to the destruction of many stands of barrel cactus.

A plant of the Sonoran and Chihuahuan deserts, this barrel is nevertheless quite frost resistant, and is thus able to grow above the desert into the surrounding mountains.

*Ferocactus wislizenii* (Engelmann) Britton & Rose
**Size:** up to 8 + feet high but usually only 4 or 5 feet
**Elevation:** 1,000–5,600 feet
**Distribution:** southern Arizona, southwestern New Mexico

# 41·CALIFORNIA BARREL

Another giant in this group is the California barrel, which is reputed to attain a height of 10 feet, but usually only reaches half that size. In central and eastern Arizona it is most commonly barrel-shaped, while in lower and eastern California it is more likely to assume a narrow cylindrical form. This barrel seldom branches.

The difference between central and radial spines is not very pronounced in this species. The centrally located spines are definitely stouter, curved, ridged, and occasionally hooked, while the other spines may be almost bristle-like. Spines are light yellow to bright red or, rarely, gray. Spination is dense and completely hides the surface of the plant, in contrast with the Arizona barrel where the green of the stems shows plainly.

The flowering season is spring or early summer. Flowers are light yellow, or occasionally light red, followed by yellow, fleshy fruits quite similar to those of the Arizona barrel.

This barrel thrives in the hot desert, usually growing in rocky soils of hillsides and canyon walls. In those parts of southern Arizona where the Arizona barrel is also found, these two barrels do not normally compete for the same space. This is because the Arizona barrel prefers to grow in less precipitous habitats where the soil is deeper.

*Ferocactus acanthodes* (Lemaire) Britton & Rose
**Size:** up to 10 feet high, usually only 5 to 6 feet
**Elevation:** 200–5,000 feet
**Distribution:** southern California, southern Nevada, southwestern Utah, southern Arizona

# 42 · SONORA BARREL

This, the third giant barrel of the Southwest, resembles the Arizona barrel when viewed from a distance. But spine clusters consist of only a few very stout spines that are all strongly cross-ridged; there are no bristle-like spines The lone central spine is very long, only slightly flattened and hooked downward. With the exception of the two white spines that extend horizontally, spines are deep red under a surface layer of gray that forms in age. This bi-color pattern also occurs in several other species of barrel cactus.

Young plants of this barrel are particularly attractive with their longer, heavier, and more deeply colored spines. The ribs of the stems are not well formed at this stage, so that spine clusters seem to stand at the end of large tubercles. The surface of the young plants is often suffused with purple. Flowers are yellow, orange, or maroon, and the fruits are similar to those of the two previous barrels. This barrel is found mainly in Sonora, Mexico, south of Arizona. In Arizona it does not occur far north of the border but is quite common in Organ Pipe Cactus National Monument, where the Arizona and California barrels are also found.

*Ferocactus covillei* Britton & Rose
**Size:** up to 8 feet high
**Elevation:** 1,500–3,500 feet
**Distribution:** south-central to southwestern Pima County, southern Yuma County, Arizona

# 43·TEXAS BARREL

Although everything is supposed to be bigger in Texas, this native rarely exceeds a foot in height. Normally green, this globe-shaped cactus frequently turns purple when in full sun or in winter. Its ribs are not continuous but seem to be made up of fused tubercles. The spines are slender, wire-like, and usually twisted in all directions giving the plant an untidy appearance. These are colored yellow, light red, or brown. The principal central spine is extremely long (up to 6 inches) and almost recurved upon itself at its tip.

Flowers are lemon-yellow, often with reddish bases while fruits are greenish-brown and so juicy that they may be used like lemons or limes.

*Ferocactus hamatacanthus* (Mühlenpfordt) Britton & Rose
**Size:** up to 1 + feet high
**Elevation:** 30–5,000 feet
**Distribution:** west Texas and along the Rio Grande to the Gulf Coast

# 44·MANY-HEADED BARREL

This dweller of the most arid regions of the Southwest does not grow tall, but it makes up for this by branching into large mounds; these blend wonderfully into the surrounding desert. There may be as many as thirty stems almost as round and as large as basketballs in one of these clumps. The curved, cross-ridged spines are dense and hide the grayish body of the stems. They are unusual in having a velvety covering on their surfaces, which partially hides the red coloration beneath. As these spines become old, they slough off this outer covering. Flowers are bright yellow, with spiny tips on the outermost petals. Dense wool covers the outside of the flowers, and stays on the developing fruits. Fruits become dry at maturity.

*Echinocactus polycephalus* Engelmann & Bigelow
**Size:** stems up to 8 or 9 inches in diameter
**Elevation:** 100–2,500 feet
**Distribution:** southern California, southern Nevada, extreme western Arizona

It is a curious and as yet not satisfactorily explained fact that this small barrel occurs in two widely separated parts of the Southwest: in south-central Arizona where it grows in a restricted area, and in southwest New Mexico and west Texas where it is widespread. In both regions it is found on limestone or soils derived from that rock. The eagle claws barrel is usually a small, globe-shaped grayish blue-green plant. Its flattened ribs are covered by very stout, curved spines, reddish to gray in color that do not hide the stems very much. In its eastern territory, this barrel rarely reaches a height of 6 inches, but in Arizona it sometimes exceeds 12 inches and may assume a columnar form. Its grayish color allows it to blend remarkably well into the surrounding gray limestone, and at first it is hard to locate it. As the eyes become attuned, more and more are discovered not far from the first one. When it blooms, its bright pink flowers at the top of the plant make it easy to spot. The flower bases are encased in a dense, white wool, as are the fruits.

*Echinocactus horizonthalonius* Lemaire
**Size:** 12 + inches high, 6 inches in diameter
**Elevation:** 2,500–5,500 feet
**Distribution:** Eastern Pima County, Arizona, southwestern New Mexico, west Texas

# 46·HORSE CRIPPLER

Riding through the grassland of Texas, many a cowboy has had his horse crippled by this low-growing barrel. It has a rigid, downward-pointing central spine ideally shaped to catch the soft underside of a hoof. Even a man walking in the grass can receive a nasty puncture. This cactus used to be plentiful, but ranchers have dug them up by the thousands by dragging chains along the ground.

Here is a cactus more tolerant of different ecological conditions than most. Witness to this is its ability to grow in the tall grass of central Texas as well as in the dry Chihuahuan Desert of west Texas.

Shaped somewhat like an inverted soup plate, the horse crippler is much wider than it is tall. It is deep green, with sharp ribs. The spines are few and all are very stout and rigid. Blooms are salmon-colored to violet, with a brightly colored throat. The petal tips are fringed and of a deeper color. They are exceptionally beautiful flowers. The fruits are woolly at first, but later lose this wool and become bright red.

*Echinocactus texensis* Höppfer
**Size:** 12 inches in diameter, 8 inches high
**Elevation:** 1,000–3,300 feet
**Distribution:** southeastern New Mexico, Big Bend of Texas, east to the vicinity of Fort Worth, south to the Gulf Coast

var. *flavidispinus*

# 47·GLORY OF TEXAS

There are two forms to this little cactus. One is larger, with fewer ribs and heavier, more brightly colored spines. In both types the ribs are made up of tubercles that are not coalesced at all in immature plants, and only partly so in mature individuals. In the smaller variety all the radial spines are yellowish; since the ribs are many, the spine cover is thick and the plant appears yellow. In the larger variety, the deep green of the plant's surface shows through. This color is set off by the almost rainbow-like aspect of the bright red and yellow spines. In addition to the radial spines, there is a heavy central spine that sticks straight out, and three to four other centrals that point up. The middle one is quite white and flattened so much that it seems paper-like in consistency. Flowers are large and satiny with a scarlet throat. Above the throat the petals are pale pink, their color gradually deepening toward their tips. This is one of the most beautiful of cactus flowers. Fruits are dry at maturity.

While common in Mexico, north of the border it occurs only in the Big Bend region of Texas and the lower Rio Grande Valley.

*Thelocactus bicolor* (Galeotti) Britton & Rose
    Vars. *flavidispinus*
          *schottii*
**Size:** 6 to 8 inches high
**Elevation:** 300–4,000 feet
**Distribution:** Big Bend of Texas and lower Rio Grande Valley.

# 48·MOJAVE PINEAPPLE CACTUS

This spiny cactus which has the shape and the size of a pineapple is formed of many ribs that are somewhat tuberculate. The numerous slightly curved, stout spines are so long that they criss-cross over each other and thus hide the surface of the cactus. These are not well differentiated into central or radial spines. The showy flowers are situated at the top of the plant.

Two forms of this species exist that are similar, except for the color of their flowers and their ecological requirements. One of these is found in the driest parts of the Mojave Desert, including the lower elevations around the Colorado river, which get very little rainfall. It also grows in the vicinity of Death Valley and southernmost Nevada. Its spine color is a pronounced pinkish-red, and its flowers are a deep pink. The other form occurs only in western Arizona, usually at higher elevations or where conditions are not so extreme. Its spines are more dully colored, and its flowers are lemon- to greenish-yellow with brownish spots at the throat. Fruits in both forms are dry at maturity.

*Echinomastus johnsonii* (Parry) Baxter
    Vars. *johnsonii*
            *lutescens*
**Size:** up to 10 inches high
**Elevation:** 1,000–4,000 feet
**Distribution:** California in the vicinity of Death Valley, southern Nevada, central-western Arizona

var. *johnsonii*

var. *lutescens*

# 49 · SONORA PINEAPPLE CACTUS

Although quite similar in shape and size to the last cactus, the Sonora pineapple grows many miles to the east in south-eastern Arizona at the upper edge of the desert. The spines are not so formidable in this species, but still do a good job in hiding the plant's surface. There is usually only one long central spine which points up and away from the body of the cactus. These central spines are quite conspicuous and give this species its name: *erectocentrus*. The color of the spines is variable but is most commonly light colored at their bases and purplish toward the tips. Flowers are light pink, sometimes almost white. Fruits are dry at maturity.

*Echinomastus erectocentrus* (Coulter) Britton & Rose
  Vars. *erectocentrus*
        *acunensis*
**Size:** up to 15 inches high
**Elevation:** 3,000–4,300 feet
**Distribution:** southeastern Arizona

var. *erectocentrus*

var. *acunensis*

# 50·CHIHUAHUA PINEAPPLE CACTUS

This, the last representative of this group, is much smaller than either the Mojave or Sonora pineapple. It is globular when young, but after it reaches approximately 3 inches in diameter it begins to elongate, finally becoming pineapple-shaped, with ribs that are often spiralled. The numerous spines are not so long that they obscure the greenish-gray body of the plant. These lie flat on the surface of the stem, with the exception of one very short central spine that sticks outward in one form of the species. In the other form all the spines stick out to some extent and are longer. Spine color is light tan, often with a purplish cast. The flowers are pale pink, almost white, with a faint purplish mid-stripe often present on the petals. This species of cactus is probably the earliest to flower. Its buds often are seen peeping through the snow cover in the northernmost part of its range as early as February. This is a plant of the Chihuahuan Desert and adjacent grasslands.

*Echinomastus intertextus* (Engelmann) Britton & Rose
　　Vars. *intertextus*
　　　　 *dasyacanthus*
**Size:** up to 6 inches high
**Elevation:** 3,000–5,500 feet
**Distribution:** southeastern Arizona, southwestern New Mexico and as far north as Albuquerque, west Texas

var. *intertextus*

The spines of this small barrel-shaped cactus are slender and somewhat angled in cross-section. The lower ones are hooked, as is the very long central spine. This central spine points up and overtops the plant body considerably so that the cactus looks as if it were imprisoned in a cage. Some of the spines are bright red, others straw-yellow. The surface of the stem is often visible and light bluish-green. The ribs seem to be formed of tubercles fused together. If you look closely at the areoles of this cactus, you will see that they extend upward as a groove. It is at the uppermost end of that groove that the flowers form. This feature is not found in the true barrels discussed earlier. As in the barrel cacti, flowers develop from areoles situated at the top of the plant. Flower color varies from orange to maroon, and fruits are bright red.

*Ancistrocactus uncinatus* (Galeotti)
L. Benson
**Size:** up to 6 inches high
**Elevation:** 3,000–4,000 feet
**Distribution:** southeastern New Mexico, west Texas

# 51 · CAT CLAW CACTUS

# 52 · CONE CACTUS

The name of this cactus comes from its resemblance to an unopened pine cone. The small green tubercles that form the surface of the plant do not quite line up into ribs. The upper surface of each tubercle is grooved from its base to the areole at its tip. Much white wool is formed along these grooves, but this wears off in age. The wooliness makes the top of the plant appear white. Each spine cluster consists of three to four light brown to black central spines, and several white, stubby radial spines which stand out conspicuously from the green of the stems. Cone cacti form small clumps. The uniformly pink blossoms of this top flowering cactus originate at the innermost end of the tubercular grooves. Fruits are dry.

*Neolloydia conoidea* (DeCandolle) Britton & Rose
**Size:** up to 4 inches high
**Elevation:** 2,300–4,000 feet
**Distribution:** west Texas

# 53·PEYOTE

Probably everyone has heard that the peyote is capable of inducing visions, while not everyone knows that it is a very pretty little cactus whose name comes from the Mexican Indian word peyotl. It also goes under the name of mescal button. Indeed it does look like a large bluish-gray button lying on the ground. Grooves along the surface of the button are often the only indication that ribs are present. In some plants ribs are formed from fused tubercles; in others, tubercles are not evident at all.

The main bulk of the cactus, which is underground, consists of a long, tuberous root that is as much as 5 inches in length. This little cactus is often single-stemmed but can form large clusters. Areoles do not bear any spines after the seedling stage, but do produce a tuft of white hairs, which contrast with the smooth gray surface of the plant. Flowers produced at the top of the plant are small and light pink. Its fruits are also small, fleshy, smooth, and red. In the past this cactus was very common in some parts of Texas, but with the advent of the craze for hallucinogenic drugs, it has become scarce.

*Lophophora williamsii* (Lemaire) Coulter
**Size:** up to 2 inches high, 3 inches across
**Elevation:** 500–4,000 feet
**Distribution:** Big Bend and lower Rio Grande Valley of Texas

Perhaps the strangest cactus you will ever see is the living rock. It does not look like a plant at all until it brings forth beautiful violet flowers from its center during the fall months. The rest of the year it merges with the gray flakes of limestone rock in which it is found. The cactus grows flush with the ground and is spineless. Its grayish triangular-shaped tubercles are warty, grooved, and fissured, characteristics that tend to break up the outline of the plant. It is easy to walk over a living rock without being aware of it at all. Once spotted, the star-shaped pattern created by the triangular outline of the tubercles becomes obvious. Suddenly you are aware of the large number of plants around you. The underground body of the plant is turnip-shaped, and wedged between the stones that form the soil. In time of severe drought, the whole cactus may shrink into the ground, be covered with sand, and thus become invisible. This is the only cactus of its kind in the United States, but south of the border there are five more species of living rocks, all of them similarly weird in aspect.

*Ariocarpus fissuratus* (Engelmann) K. Schumann
**Size:** up to 3 inches across
**Elevation:** 1,650–3,900 feet
**Distribution:** Big Bend of Texas and lower Rio Grande Valley

*Epithelantha micromeris*

# 55 · BUTTON CACTUS

This tiny cactus looks like a miniature puffball mushroom. The tubercles are minuscule and completely hidden underneath the profusion of tiny spines. There are two species of button cactus which resemble each other closely enough as to make identification difficult. Spine clusters of buttons are so small that they merge into either a rough or smooth white surface, depending on which of the two species you are looking at. With age, the spines break off in the middle. Spines of the "rough" button cactus break unevenly, with a corresponding rough appearance of the plant. In the case of the "smooth" button cactus, they break off evenly, resulting in a satiny smooth surface. These little gems branch, but do not often form large clumps.

The light pink flowers are found at the very center of the plants. On the rough button, they are so inconspicuous that they are hard to see, while flowers of the smooth button are a little larger. The fruits on the other hand are long, bright red, and edible.

In times of drought, the plants lose their plump appearance and the center of the cactus becomes shrunken. Both button cacti grow best in full sun and soil derived from limestone rock.

*Epithelantha bokei* L. Benson (Smooth Button Cactus)
**Size:** ½ to 1½ + inches in diameter
**Elevation:** 2,500–4,000 feet
**Distribution:** Big Bend of Texas

*Epithelantha micromeris* (Engelmann) Weber (Rough Button Cactus)
**Size:** ½ to 2½ + inches in diameter
**Elevation:** 3,400–5,800 feet
**Distribution:** southeastern Arizona to west Texas

# CORYPHANTHA & ESCOBARIA
## (*Pincushions*)

Here we have left the domain of ribbed cacti; this group is composed of plants that have tubercles only. These are grooved on the upper surface, this groove running from the base of the tubercle to the spine bearing areole (figure 3). It is at the very top of the plant, and always at the end of the groove farthest from the spines, that flowers originate. The blooms are large, most commonly yellow, but occasionally pink or violet in the case of Coryphanthas; in Escobarias they are small and light to deep pink.

Fruits are smooth, thin skinned and juicy. Those of Coryphanthas are green or yellow, the size and shape of elongated grapes; those of Escobarias are smaller, elongated and usually reddish.

Coryphanthas are in general bigger rounded plants with large tubercles, stouter spines and in many cases are not hidden by their spines. Escobarias are cylindrical or egg-shaped with a large number of quite small and thin spines. The spines, most often translucent white, completely hide the surface of the plants.

Unfortunately, there are some species that seem to fall half way between these two genera. The spiny star is an example.

*Coryphantha vivipara* var. *bisbeeana*

# 56·GIANT PINCUSHION

As the name implies, this cactus is of large proportions. Its beehive shape and its heavy hooked central spine give it the appearance of a small barrel. But the large tubercles (nearly 1 inch long) with upper grooved surfaces help to identify it as a Coryphantha. The stout, but not numerous, spines only partially hide the surface of the plant, which is green to grayish-green. The spines are ivory sometimes tinged with rust, especially at the tips. Flowers are large, and yellow to orange-yellow.

South of Tucson it is widespread but only occurs as solitary individuals widely separated from their neighbors and not easy to find. The form occurring in that region has few, but especially stout spines. Most plants are single-stemmed, but old individuals will sometimes form offsets at their bases. These new shoots develop their own root system so that if the mother plant dies, these offsets will survive. Plants growing in extreme southeastern Arizona, New Mexico, and west Texas have more numerous, but slenderer spines.

var. *valida*

*Coryphantha scheeri* Lemaire
    Vars. *scheeri*
        *robustispina*
        *valida*
**Size:** up to 9 + inches high, 5 + inches in diameter
**Elevation:** 2,300–5,000 feet
**Distribution:** southeastern Pima County, Santa Cruz County, Arizona to west Texas

var. *robustispina*

# 57·GOLDEN PINCUSHION

It is exciting to come across the golden pincushion, which is only found in a small area near the Mexico border in Santa Cruz County, Arizona. Its large, round stems, up to 6 inches across, nestle tightly together to form golden mounds. These have been known to measure more than 3 feet across and contain as many as fifty stems. Plants of this size are now rare because collectors in past years could not resist digging them up to put in their gardens.

The light green surface of the plant barely shows through the dense covering of short yellow spines. The radial spines are recurved inward while the one to two central spines curve downward as well as outward. Due to the spine arrangement the plants have a well-groomed appearance. This Coryphantha's mode of flowering is not typical: its yellow flowers emerge close to, but not at the top of the plant. Unfortunately this species is an infrequent bloomer, so few people have been lucky enough to see it in flower.

This attractive cactus grows on rocky or grassy hillsides. A good area to see it is along the Ruby Road and at Sycamore Canyon just northwest of Nogales.

*Coryphantha recurvata* (Engelmann) Britton & Rose
**Size:** stems to 6 inches across, mounds to 3 feet across
**Elevation:** 4,000–6,000 feet
**Distribution:** Santa Cruz County, Arizona

# 58·FLABBY PINCUSHION

This untidy looking cactus often forms mats or low mounds along sandy areas or rocky hills in the desert. There it prefers the protection of shrubs. It is flabby from its fleshy taproot to its long, upward-curving tubercles. There are two to eight, dark brown to black central spines; radial spines have a slightly higher count and are white or gray. The spines are long, angled in cross section, and point in all directions. The surface of the plant is hardly obscured by the spines; it varies in color from gray to green. Grooves of the tubercles are short in this species and give rise to both flowers and branches.

If this cactus looks forlorn much of the time, it makes up for it when it produces its beautiful blooms which are violet and large with fringed or toothed petals.

This is a common plant from around Las Cruces, New Mexico, down to the Big Bend country of Texas.

*Coryphantha macromeris* (Engelmann) Orcutt
**Size:** to 6 inches high
**Elevation:** 2,500–4,500 feet
**Distribution:** south-central to southeastern New Mexico, west Texas

Unlike the flabby pincushion, the Texas pincushion has a firm body with a trim and neat appearance. It forms small to large clusters. Each of the stems is globular or slightly elongated. Its dense covering of radial spines, which lie more or less flat against the stem, effectively hides the surface of the plant. The principal central spine is quite stout and long, and sticks straight out, giving the plant its typical character. All spines are ivory to pale yellow turning gray with age, but spine tips are sometimes brownish.

Juvenile plants or those growing under adverse conditions do not develop any central spines and therefore have a radically different look to them. In the past they were thought to represent a different species of Coryphantha.

Flowers are large and bright yellow; petals are toothed at their tips, and have a sharp terminal point. The striking feature of these blooms is their red stamens, which give the impression of a bright red center.

This cactus is restricted to west Texas, where it usually grows under the protection of shrubs.

*Coryphantha echinus* (Engelmann) Britton & Rose
**Size:** 4 inches high, 2½ inches in diameter
**Elevation:** 2,200–4,800 feet
**Distribution:** west Texas

# 60·SPINY STARS

Southwestern varieties of the spiny stars are densely spine-covered, the surface of the cactus not being visible at all. Most of the varieties form small to large mounds consisting of globular or slightly elongated stems. Juvenile individuals have only white radial spines which lie flat against the stems, and so look smooth, tidy and light colored. As the plants mature, central spines develop that are stouter, longer, outward pointing and white to brown. Adult cacti have a slightly bristly appearance and may be all white or brownish.

Flowers of all the varieties (except vars. *buoflama* and *desertii*) are large, wide open, light to deep pink or violet. The two above mentioned exceptions have small flowers that are bell-shaped and are either yellow, peach or rust-colored.

This species consists of a great number of varieties spread over a large region of the western United States, western Canada and northern Mexico. Only one of these varieties has colonized the northern states and Canada; it is not found in our area. Most of the varieties growing in the Southwest are found in the higher elevations of the desert although some of these range into the mountains as well. Variety *rosea* on the other hand grows only in the mountains. All spiny stars are quite winter hardy.

var. *buoflama*

*Coryphantha vivipara* (Nuttall) Britton & Rose
    Vars. *bisbeeana*
          *buoflama*
          *desertii*
          *neo-mexicana*
          *rosea*

**Size:** 3 to 8 inches high, 2½ to 4 inches in diameter
**Elevation:** 2,950–9,000 feet
**Distribution:** southern California, to west Texas

var. *bisbeeana*

*Escobaria tuberculosa*

# 61·WHITE STARS

These predominantly white pincushions are found throughout the southernmost parts of New Mexico and in west Texas. Each mountain range seems to have its own variation of this cactus and are quite difficult to tell apart.

Essentially these plants are egg-shaped or are short and cylindrical with numerous, small tubercles; these are hidden by a large number of quite short, central and radial spines similar to each other, somewhat translucent and off-white in color. Some varieties are single-stemmed while others form clumps. Unlike spiny stars, white stars have small pale pink-colored blossoms. Fruits are usually red or reddish-brown. This cactus grows in rocky areas and in cracks between rocks in preference to other habitats.

White stars and spiny stars resemble each other, but spiny stars' stems are more rounded in shape. In parts of the Southwest, where these two cacti grow close, spiny stars have flowers that are much larger and more deeply colored.

*Escobaria tuberculosa* (Engelmann) Britton & Rose
**Size:** up to 7 inches high, 2½ inches in diameter
**Elevation:** 2,500–5,000 feet
**Distribution:** southern border of Arizona and New Mexico, southern New Mexico, west Texas

*Escobaria dasyacantha* (Engelmann) Britton & Rose
**Size:** up to 7 inches high, 2½ inches in diameter
**Elevation:** 2,700–5,800 feet
**Distribution:** west Texas

# MAMMILLARIA
## (*Pincushions and Fishhooks*)

The genus *Mammillaria* is one of the largest in the cactus family, with Mexico having the largest number of different species.

Unlike Coryphanthas and Escobarias, Mammillarias do not have grooved tubercles, nor do the flowers form at the very top of the plant; rather they originate at the base of tubercles which were produced the previous year. As the tubercles of the same age lie in a circle around the stem, blossoms occur in rings. Fruits are smooth, fleshy, and often bright red in this genus.

Mammillarias can be grouped into species that have only straight spines (pincushions), and those whose central spines are hooked at their tips (fishhooks). Occasional individuals of most species of fishhooks do not develop hooks on their spines.

*Mammillaria dioica*

var. *macdougalii*

# 62 · CREAM PINCUSHION

You will not find this attractive plant in the low desert. It grows at higher elevations where rainfall is somewhat more plentiful. In the mountain foothills of southeastern Arizona it occurs in rocky areas usually in full sun.

You could easily walk over this cactus without being aware of the fact, since it usually grows perfectly flat on the surface of the ground. Should one of these plants chance to grow under the shade of a shrub, its shape will be rounded rather than flat; this shows the dependence of form on the amount of incident sunlight.

Like all cacti in this group, the small clusters of spines grow from the tips of tubercles that make up the surface of the plant. If you should prick one of these tubercles with a needle (during the growing season especially), white latex will ooze out:

this is the only cactus growing in the United States that has milky sap. In the late spring, a ring of pale yellow flowers forms around the center of the cactus in variety *macdougalii* followed later by red fruits. There are two other varieties of this pincushion with pinkish flowers; these are found in New Mexico and Texas. (Varieties *meiacantha* and *heyderi*).

*Mammillaria heyderi* Mühlenfordt
   Vars. *heyderi*
        *macdougalii*
        *meiacantha*
**Size:** to 6 inches across
**Elevation:** 3,500–6,000 feet
**Distribution:** south-central Arizona to west Texas

# 63·LACYSPINE PINCUSHION

This diminutive, usually single-stemmed cactus looks like a golf ball and rarely grows any larger. Its tiny tubercles are covered with clusters of minute, snow-white, bristly spines that are all alike and number between forty and eighty per cluster. (Many of these are finely hairy, but a hand lens is needed to see this). Spines from neighboring areoles interlace and do not allow any view of the plant surface. Because these spines lie flat it is possible to handle the plants with complete safety.

This pincushion grows in the same areas as the button cactus and since they are similar in appearance, the two cacti are easily mistaken for one another. The lacyspine pincushion flowers originate, not at the apex of the plant as with the button cactus, but close to the top; they are also much larger, sometimes even hiding the plant body. Their petals are rounded at the tips, whitish with a tan, brown or reddish mid-stripe. Fruits are long and red.

The lacyspine pincushion grows in full sun, its dense spine covering acting as an efficient sun shade. It requires rocky soils of limestone origin.

*Mammillaria lasiacantha* Engelmann
**Size:** up to 2 inches across
**Elevation:** 3,000–4,300 feet
**Distribution:** southeastern New Mexico, west Texas

# *64*·THIN PINCUSHION

The range of this small pincushion is restricted to the Big Bend region of Texas, where it grows in limestone soils. It differs from all the other members of this group (Mammillaria) found in the United States, because it is quite tall and very thin. Sometimes it is single-stemmed, but it often forms small clusters. The spines are dense (as many as forty radial spines per cluster) and rigid. The radial spines are pale in color and obscure almost completely the surface of the stem. The several central spines are more highly colored, being purplish, brownish, or rust-colored. They radiate out in all directions except for the uppermost spine, which is much longer and points upward, making it the most conspicuous of all the spines.

Flowers arise near the top of the plant and are quite small, barely protruding from between the spines, but their bright orange-red, red, or even purplish-red color delights the eye. Fruits are long and red.

*Mammillaria pottsii* Engelmann
**Size:** up to 8 inches high, almost 2 inches in diameter
**Elevation:** 2,500–3,000 feet
**Distribution:** Big Bend region of Texas

# 65·MANY-SPINED FISHHOOK

You must travel to the drier parts of the western Arizona and southern California deserts to see this cactus, as it cannot tolerate much moisture.

Plants are most commonly single-stemmed and grow far apart, so that seeing one is no assurance of finding another one.

The radial spines are especially slender and so numerous (forty to sixty per cluster) that they hide the surface of the plant completely. They are usually snow-white but sometimes have dark red tips. The central spines are also numerous and a little heavier, dark red to black, and very long. Commonly, as many as four of them per areole are hooked. The many hooked centrals, standing out from a background of many white radials gives this species its characteristic appearance.

Blossoms are very large (almost 2 inches across;) the throat of the flower is deep pink and the petals are light pink with a deeper mid-stripe. Fruits are long and bright red.

*Mammillaria tetrancistra* Engelmann
**Size:** up to 6 inches high, 2½ inches in diameter
**Elevation:** 450–3,000+ feet
**Distribution:** southern California, southern Nevada, western Arizona

# *66·*ARIZONA FISHHOOK

More moisture tolerant than the many-spined fishhook, this species ranges from western Arizona to New Mexico where rainfall is more plentiful. Most commonly it grows under the shade of shrubs or trees. While similar to the many-spined fishhook in general appearance, its radial spines are fewer and only one of its central spines is hooked. It is globular to cylindrical in shape. Central spines in this species are dark red to black, but occasionally plants with light colored spines are encountered.

Flowers are similar in color to those of the many-spined fishhook, but are quite a bit smaller. Fruits are long and bright red.

There are two forms of this cactus: variety *microcarpa* grows further west and is restricted to the desert while variety *grahamii* occurs in the desert and also at higher elevations. Variety *microcarpa* is taller with heavier and longer central spines. Its pale radial spines are few and do not hide the surface of the stem completely while variety *grahamii's* many more radial spines are more consistently white.

Often among the plants of variety *grahamii* individuals are found that have not developed normal hooked central spines; instead a straight nubbin sticks outward. Plants having such abnormal spines look quite different from usual plants and have been thought to represent a different species by some botanists.

Where this species grows in the same places as the many-spined fishhook, the two species occasionally hybridize making certain identification difficult.

*Mammillaria microcarpa* Engelmann
  Vars. *microcarpa*
        *grahamii*
**Size:** up to 6 inches high
**Elevation:** 1,000–5,500 feet
**Distribution:** southern Arizona to west Texas

var. *grahamii*

var. *microcarpa*

# 67·LITTLE FISHHOOK CACTUS

The small size of this fishhook is offset by its propensity for clustering. It will grow only where it is shaded from the full sun. This can be under shrubs and frequently at the base of jumping chollas where the germinating seeds find added protection provided by the numerous fallen cholla joints. Clusters of plants are made up of many individual stems that blend amazingly well into their surroundings.

Stem dimensions are small compared to those of the many-spined and Arizona fishhooks, Moreover this fishhook is proportionately thinner for its height than the other species. Radial spines are few and do not hide the green surface of the stems completely; they are white with reddish tips. There is only one central spine, which is light tan with a light reddish hooked tip.

Flowers have fewer petals than other fishhook cacti. These are light to deep pink. The most striking feature of the flowers is the deep magenta stigmas. Fruits are long and bright red.

*Mammillaria thornberi* Orcutt
**Size:** up to 4 inches tall, 1 inch in diameter
**Elevation:** 800–3,300 feet
**Distribution:** Pima County, Arizona as far east as Tucson, South of Tucson, and western Maricopa County, Arizona

# 68·COAST FISHHOOK

This fishhook is mostly a coastal species, occurring from the vicinity of San Diego down the Baja California peninsula, but is also found in the extreme western part of the Colorado Desert of southern California.

In its desert habitat it often forms small clumps. It is a stout, cylindrical plant with many crowded tubercles. Radial spines are relatively few and light colored, and not so dense as to obscure the green surface of the stems completely. There are two or three straight, and one hooked, central spine which is red to dark brown. These centrals are usually shorter than those of the other species of fishhooks.

This cactus has one unusual feature: short bristles that grow out of the bases of the tubercles, at the same places where flower buds originate. The few-petaled flowers are pale yellow with a faint to pronounced red mid-stripe. Fruits are long, fat, and red.

*Mammillaria dioica* K. Brandegee
**Size:** 6 inches high, 2½ inches in diameter
**Elevation:** 1,000–5,000 feet in Colorado Desert
**Distribution:** San Diego; eastern San Diego County, southwestern Imperial County in southern California

# 69·LARGE-FRUITED FISHHOOK

This small, flaccid, globular cactus grows from just above the upper limit of the desert into grassland, woodland, and even in the pine belt. Stems are light to dark green and usually single in this species. Radial spines are very fine and all white or white with brownish tips. Central spines are long, dark colored, all hooked, and may number as many as seven or as few as one.

Blooms are a spectacular deep violet to magenta and are commonly 2 inches across, but may reach 3 inches. The plants flower in late summer. The fruits are the largest in this group of cacti, about the size and shape of a grape, green to purplish.

*Mammillaria wrightii* Engelmann
    Vars. *wrightii*
              *wilcoxii*
**Size:** 3 inches in diameter
**Elevation:** 3,500–8,000 feet
**Distribution:** southeastern Arizona and New Mexico

var. *wilcoxii*

# 70 · GREEN-FLOWERED FISHHOOK

In spite of its name, the bell-shaped flowers of this fishhook are not actually green, but range from greenish-yellow to peach, salmon, and occasionally pink. Its profusion of bloom in the spring make up for the small size of its blossoms.

Stems are most commonly globular, flaccid and do not cluster much. The fine radial spines are white and dense. The one to four central spines are fine, long, and hooked, light orange to dark brown. Fruits are greenish-brown and oblong.

The green-flowered fishhook makes its home from the upper edge of the desert into the mountains where it usually grows in soils of granitic origin. Where isolated mountain ranges rise out of the southern Arizona desert, it is sure to occur at upper elevations.

The green-flowered and large-fruited fishhooks are difficult to differentiate when they are not in flower or fruit. The latter has very large and deeply colored flowers with much larger fruits. It often has more central hooked spines, but this is not a reliable trait, so it is best not to try to tell them apart without seeing their blossoms and fruits.

*Mammillaria viridiflora* (Britton & Rose) Bödeker
**Size:** up to 3 inches in diameter
**Elevation:** 3,000–8,000 feet
**Distribution:** northwestern, central-western to southeastern Arizona, southwestern New Mexico

# GLOSSARY

**areole:** specialized area found in all cacti, from which spines, branches and flowers originate

**bristle:** a very rigid hair

**burr:** a fruit thickly covered with spines

**central spine(s):** the heavier, more pigmented spine(s) found in the center of the spine clusters

**deciduous:** falling away at the end of the growing season as the leaves in trees

**endemic:** occurring naturally in only a restricted geographical area

**epiphyte:** growing on another plant but not obtaining its sustenance from that plant

**felted:** with intertwined matted hair

**genus:** a group of closely related species

**glochid:** small barbed bristle occurring in the areoles of *Opuntia*

**habit:** the general form of a plant

**habitat:** the locality and the type of environmental condition where a plant normally grows

**joint:** the name often applied to the individual branches of *Opuntia*

**latex:** opaque, milky and often gummy juice produced by some plants of the genus *Mammillaria* (in the cactus family); also found in other plant families

**nurse plant:** plant under whose protective shade seedlings (of cacti) often grow

**ovary:** lowest part of the pistil where ovules, and later, seeds are formed

**pad:** the name often applied to the individual branches of prickly pears

**pectinate:** arranged like the teeth of a comb

**perianth:** sepals and petals collectively

**proliferous:** flower arising from the areole of an already formed fruit

**radial spine(s):** the spine(s) which surround the central spine in a cluster (usually thinner and less pigmented)

**stigma:** the upper end of the pistil which is receptive to pollen

**succulent:** with much soft watery tissue—fleshy

**tubercle:** protuberance found in some groups of cacti, usually terminated by a spine cluster at its tip

**tuberculate:** having tubercles

**tuberous:** like a potato tuber: a thickened underground root or stem

**turgid:** swollen (with water)

**variety:** a subdivision of species, i.e. a species may consist of several varieties.

# SUGGESTED READING

Benson, Lyman. 1969. *The Cacti of Arizona* 3d ed. Tucson: University of Arizona Press.

———. 1969. *The Native Cacti of California*. Stanford: Stanford University Press.

———. 1970. The Cactaceae [of Texas] In C.L. Lundell et. al. *The Flora of Texas*. Renner: Texas Research Foundation. (also printed separately)

———. 1982 *The Cacti of the United States and Canada*, Stanford: Stanford University Press.

Champie, Clark. [ ]. *Cacti & Succulents of El Paso*. Santa Barbara, CA: Abbey Garden Press

Lamb, Edgar, and Brian Lamb. 1974. *Colorful Cacti of the American Southwest*. NY: Macmillan.

Shreve, Forrest, and Ira L. Wiggins. 1964. *Vegetation and Flora of the Sonoran Desert*. Stanford: Stanford University Press.

Weniger, Del. 1970. *Cacti of the Southwest*. Austin: University of Texas Press.

# INDEX

# ACKNOWLEDGMENTS

I want to thank the following people who have critically read this manuscript and made many helpful suggestions: my wife, Constance Lindsay; Dr. Charles T. Mason, Jr.; Mr. Robert Ellis; Mrs. Mary MacEwan; and Mrs. Marie Burling.

ISBN 0-911408-82-7

20161

$ 695